Oh My Baby Girl

James Jaskolski

AuthorHouse™
1663 Liberty Drive
Bloomington, IN 47403
www.authorhouse.com
Phone: 833-262-8899

Because of the dynamic nature of the Internet, any web addresses or links contained in this book may have changed since publication and may no longer be valid. The views expressed in this work are solely those of the author and do not necessarily reflect the views of the publisher, and the publisher hereby disclaims any responsibility for them.

Interior Image Credit: James Jaskolski

This book is printed on acid-free paper.

ISBN: 978-1-6655-7144-9 (sc)
ISBN: 978-1-6655-7146-3 (hc)
ISBN: 978-1-6655-7145-6 (e)

Print information available on the last page.

Published by AuthorHouse 10/06/2022

authorHOUSE®

By Jamie Jaskolski

To Venezia

Follow
Your
Dream

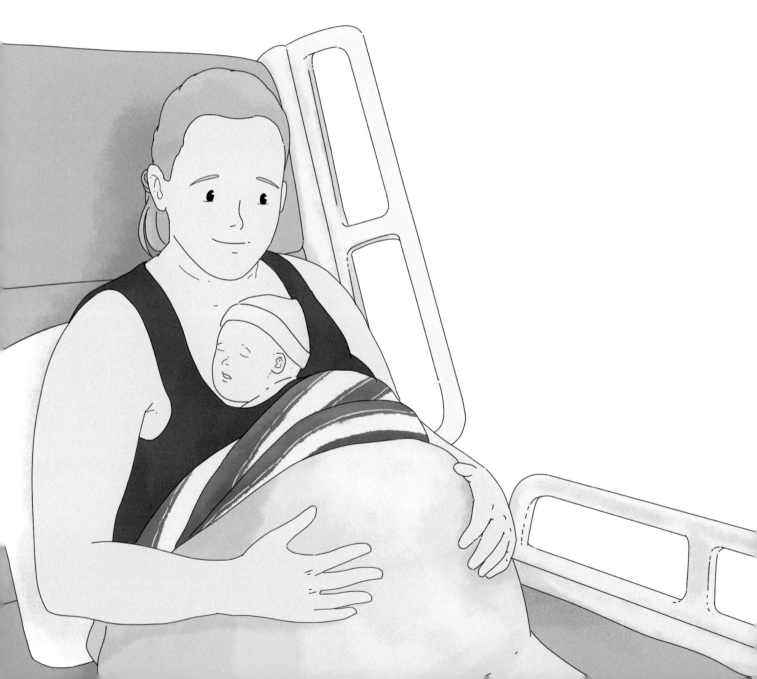

Oh My Baby Girl

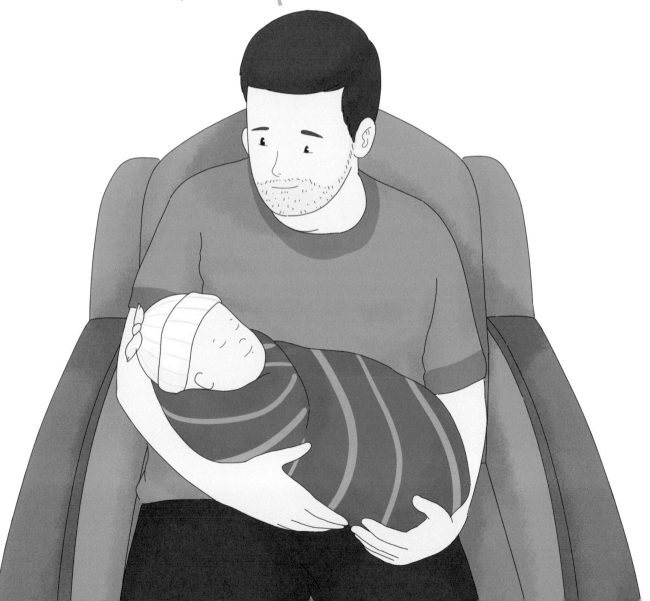

Oh My Baby Girl

I'll take away all
of your fears

And Oh My Baby Girl

I'll love You
with all that I have

And Oh My Baby Girl

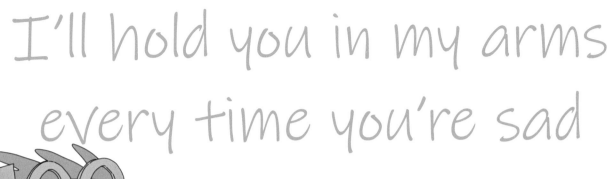

I'll hold you in my arms
every time you're sad

with every second
of every minute

And every hour
of every day

Of all the people in
this great big world

I'll love you the most
my Beautiful Baby Girl

The End

Printed in the United States
by Baker & Taylor Publisher Services